A Kin/Der Owl Book

Holt, Rinehart and Winston, Inc.

New York, Toronto, London

Buzz, *Buzz,* *Buzzing*
BEES

by Gene Fulks

with pictures by Zena Bernstein

It is early in the morning.
The bees are waking up.
Flights of worker bees are swarming
out of the beehive.
Buzz . . . buzz . . . buzz.
They are on their way to work.

The worker bees fly . . .
buzz . . . buzz . . . buzzing . . .
       up, up,
       over the tree,
       over the meadows,
       over the fields of clover,
       across the river,
       straight to the orange grove,
       far, far away.
They fly so far away from the beehive,
so far away from home.
Oh, how will they find their long way back?

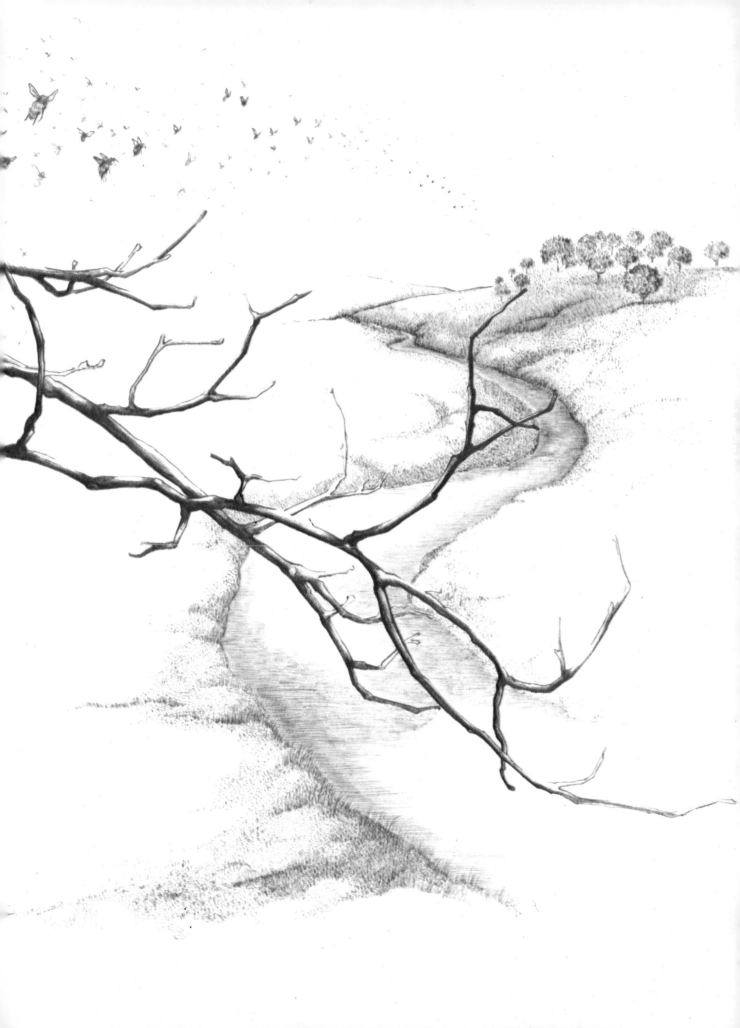

Buzz . . . buzz . . . buzz.
Thousands of worker bees
swarm down into the orange trees,
swarm down into the sweetness
of the sweet white orange blossoms.
Burrowing deep into the blossoms,
they gather the sweet nectar
and buzz from blossom to blossom,
buzz . . . buzz . . . buzzing.
Their honey sacks, now filled with nectar,
their pollen baskets bulging with golden pollen,
the worker bees fly homeward,
carrying their heavy loads.

With eyes as keen as the eyes of a bird,
they see the bend in the river,
they see the fence through the clover,
they see the tree in the meadow,
and they see the narrow little lane
that leads them back to the beehive.
The worker bees never get lost.
The worker bees always come home.

Buzz . . . buzz . . . buzz.
The worker bees are crawling back into the beehive,
unloading the sweet nectar from their honey sacs
and the golden pollen from their pollen baskets.
Most of the worker bees are ready to go
*   to the orange grove again*
but some will not return.
Weary with work,
their wings tattered and torn,
some drop to the floor of the hive and die.
But the work goes on.
Other worker bees take their places
and swarm out of the beehive
*   to fly toward the orange grove.*
The endless search for nectar and golden pollen
*   goes on and on and on.*
Buzz . . . buzz . . . buzz.

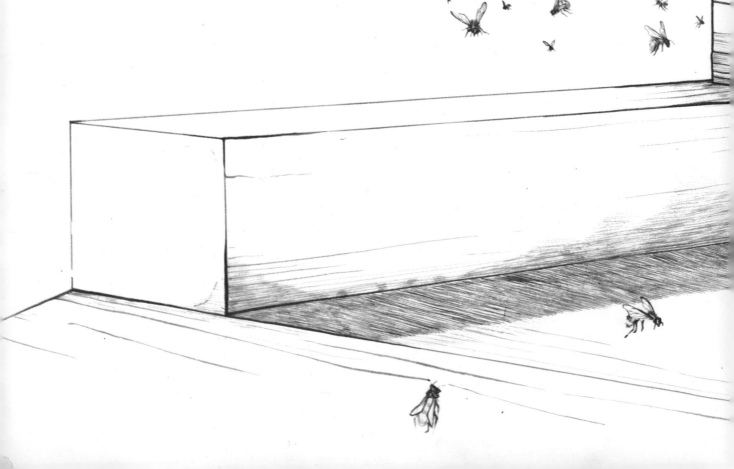

But back inside the beehive,
thousands of other worker bees
are swarming over the honeycomb,
turning the nectar from the orange
    blossoms into honey,
chewing the golden pollen to feed the baby bees,
making wax from some of the nectar
    to build the honeycomb,
buzz . . . buzz . . . buzzing.
So many bees you couldn't count them all,
all of them busy from morning till dark—
all except the drone bees.

The drone bees are men bees.
They keep the queen bee company.
They dawdle around the beehive,
begging the busy nurse bees for droplets of honey,
    pestering,
    begging
    and buzzing
    all day long.
One of the drone bees
will one day marry the queen bee
and become the father of new baby bees.

But back inside the beehive,
thousands of other worker bees
are swarming over the honeycomb,
turning the nectar from the orange
blossoms into honey,
chewing the golden pollen to feed the baby bees,
making wax from some of the nectar
to build the honeycomb,
buzz . . . buzz . . . buzzing.
So many bees you couldn't count them all,
all of them busy from morning till dark—
all except the drone bees.

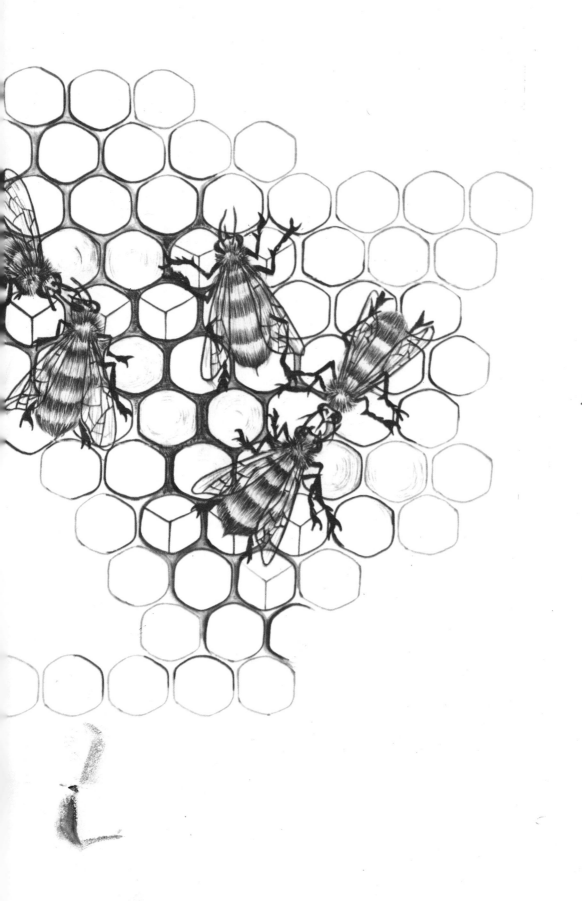

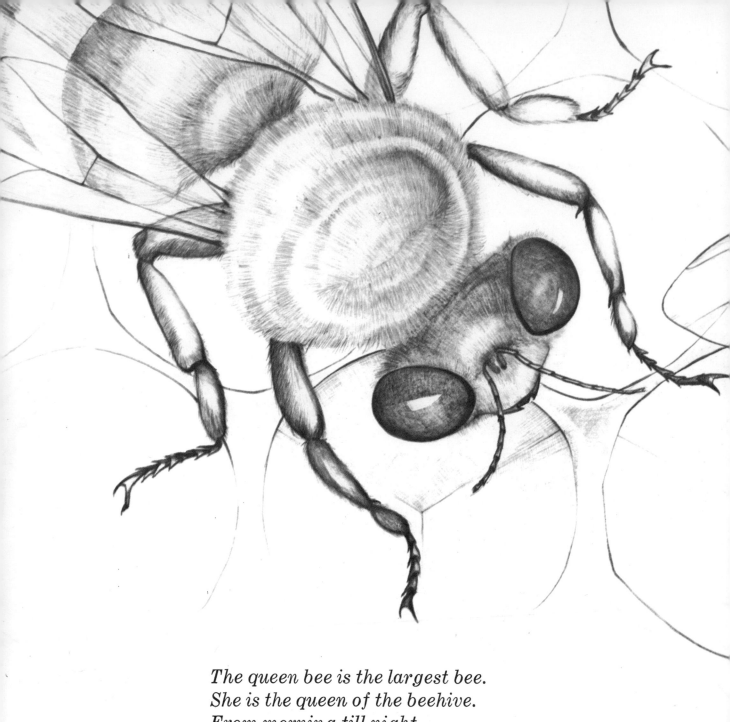

The queen bee is the largest bee.
She is the queen of the beehive.
From morning till night,
after she is married,
she crawls over the honeycomb
laying eggs to hatch baby bees.
The queen bee is a busy bee.
She sometimes lays 4,000 eggs in a day.
4,000 eggs . . . 4,000 baby bees.
Buzz . . . buzz . . . buzz.

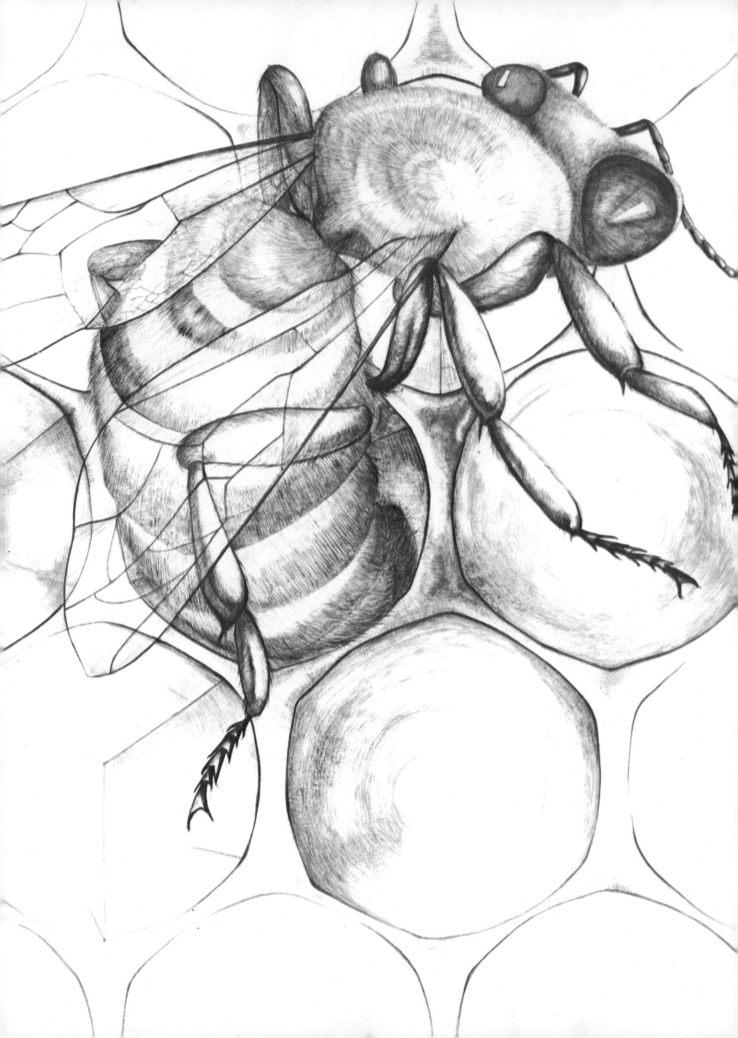

The nurse bees go right to work
      caring for the newborn babies.
The babies are hungry.
They must be fed and tended by the nurse bees
until the babies are four days old.
Then the baby bees, like other bees,
become workers in the beehive.
One day, they, too, will swarm out of the beehive,
buzz . . . buzz . . . buzzing,
straight to the orange grove.

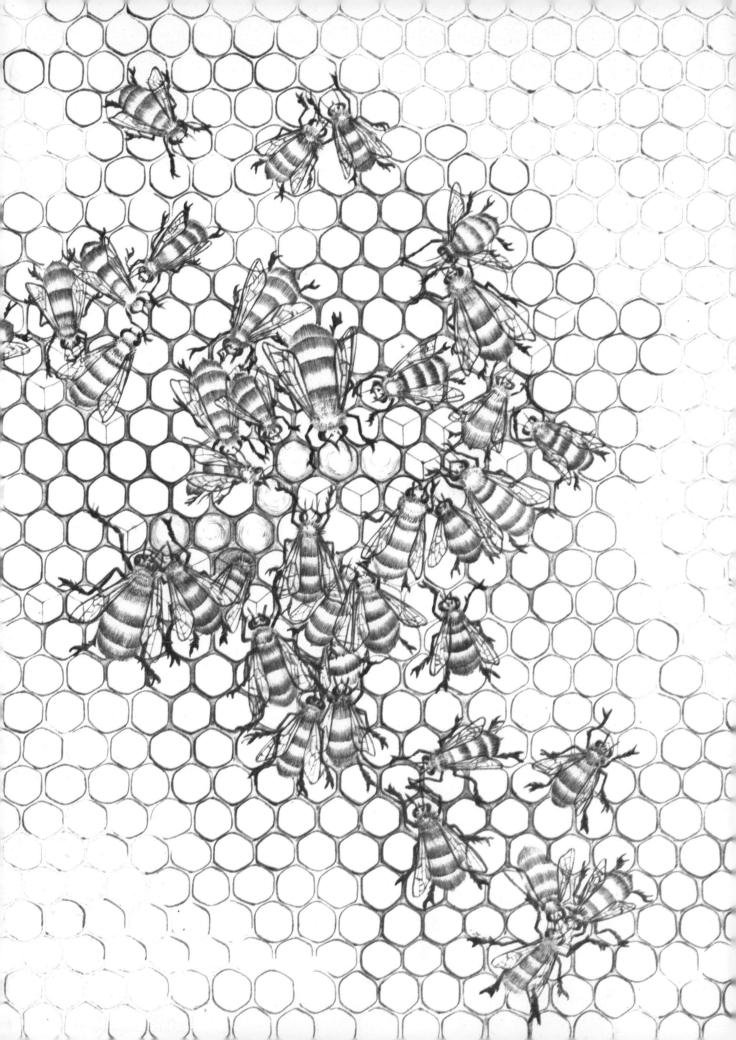

Step . . . step . . . step.
A beekeeper is coming down the narrow lane.
He wears heavy gloves and a netting over his hat.
He is coming to rob the beehive of its
    rich golden honey.
Step . . . step . . . step.
The beekeeper is walking away
with a bucketful of rich golden honey.

And still there comes another intruder.
Scratch . . . scratch . . . scratch.
A mother skunk and her four kittens
    have come to the beehive.
They have come at night
when the bees cannot fly and sting them.
Oh how wise, Mother Skunk!
Scratch . . . scratch . . . scratch.
The bees stir but they do not fly.
They do not fly at night
because they cannot see their way in the dark.
The bees, sensing the danger,
    crawl out of the beehive to see who is there.
Snap . . . snap . . . snap.
The skunks eat until they are full.

1562707

But soon it will be morning.
And soon there will be more nectar
and more honey and more eggs and more bees.
The endless making of honey
goes on and on and on.
Buzz . . . buzz . . . buzz.